Tiny BOOK of MAGIC

Tiny BOOK of MAGIC

A GENIE'S GUIDE TO A WISHES FULFILLED LIFE

JOSHUA PAUL DAWSON

TINY BOOK OF MAGIC

A Genie's Guide to a Wishes Fulfilled Life

Copyright © 2016 by Joshua Paul Dawson

TINY BOOK OF MAGIC is a registered trademark of Joshua Paul Dawson

Cover Design: Azmat Ullah

© 2016 Joshua Paul Dawson

North Charleston, SC

ISBN-10: 153960957X

ISBN-13: 978-1539609575

Library of Congress Control Number: 2016915283

I learned this, at least, by my experiment; that if one advances confidently in the direction of his dreams, and endeavors to live the life which he has imagined, he will meet with a success unexpected in common hours.

- Henry David Thoreau

CONTENTS

Acknowledgements   vii

Introduction   1

CHAPTER 1
The Illusion of Death   13

CHAPTER 2
The Illusion of Force   29

CHAPTER 3
The Illusion of Secrecy   39

CHAPTER 4
The Illusion of Hardship   51

CHAPTER 5
The Illusion of Limitations   65

CHAPTER 6
The Illusion of Ownership   95

CHAPTER 7
The Illusion of Time   109

Tiny Book of Magic
Reminders   121

About the Author   127

ACKNOWLEDGEMENTS

This book has been a labor of love over a period of seven years, with many people to thank. I would like to express my sincere gratitude to the following people for helping bring this *Tiny Book of Magic* out of hiding:

Ingrid Thornhill, beauty personified, a partner and soul mate whose life guidance leads me deeper into the understanding of love every day.

My biggest teachers and loving sons, Jack and Hugo Dawson, for helping me see the beauty of magic.

Gayle Dawson, for being such a real mom. Showing me the strength to follow my heart with conviction, while always having my back. I love you dearly.

Hollie, Matt, and Nick Dawson, for putting up with their big brother. I love you more than I let on sometimes.

Rich Olexa, Allison Brown, and Wilson Brown, for their unfaltering support and understanding when it was needed most.

Colleen May, for reminding me to believe in a higher truth and always lending an ear to these writings when they first began to bloom.

Bill Thornhill, for his unique way of revealing that this moment is all we truly have.

Wayne Dyer's editor, Joanna Pyle, for graciously offering to edit this book.

Dr. Wayne Dyer, Deepak Chopra, Marianne Williamson, James Van Praagh, Gabrielle Bernstein, Jack Canfield, Eckhart Tolle, and all the people I've met on this genie journey for the noble, conscious, transformational inspiration.

My Dad, for showing the way.

With love,

Josh

INTRODUCTION

It ain't what you don't know that gets you in trouble. It's what you know for sure that just ain't so.

- Mark Twain

I am a genie. Well, let's be a bit more precise. I dress like one while granting wishes to people in need. I am also homeless. Have been almost six years. But not in the way you may now be visualizing. My homelessness is a little more deliberate. On October 4, 2010, my partner, Ingrid, and I walked out of our comfortable life, jumped into a black Grand Prix, and began a journey into the unknown. Following our hearts.

Ask my kids where Daddy lives, and they'll say "everywhere" without missing a beat. And in that regard, they're absolutely right. I have no fixed address, traveling to exciting destinations, shining a light where needed. Many people see only the gloss of this life and think it's all happy faces and smooth sailing. It's not. The truth is, we've worked incredibly hard to get to this point. Changing the momentum of your life isn't a cakewalk. It takes a lot of practice and effort to adjust your conditioned way of thinking. Courage is needed to trust your gut, especially when so many think you're crazy for going against the grain. Doing things differently. If you're interested in comfort, you might as well stop reading now.

Is our life easy? Not at all. Have we pushed the limits of our relationship, pocketbook, and sanity to transform? Yes. We've taken buses to wish grants with only one hundred dollars left to our names and slept on friends' and families' couches more times than I can count. I've quit more than once, only to change my mind the next day. Why? Something in me kept saying, "Don't give up. Take one more step." And always, at the right time, something needed would appear. Imminent failures magically avoided at that last moment.

The first few years were exciting but hard. "Fifty pounds or less" is our running joke because that's the extent of our belongings—fifty pounds each. If we go over, we're punished by the airlines with a baggage penalty. Keeping us (and the bags) in check. Downsizing from owning a house, car, and all life's standard fixings takes a bit of getting used to. Never knowing where the money might come from or where we might be sleeping from one night to the next isn't for the faint of heart. It's a faith-guided tightrope-balancing act.

Today, life on the road is normal for us. Things we once considered disasters are now opportunities to learn more about ourselves. But we had to learn to walk before we could run. With this new balance, we now surf the waves of life, going with the flow, trusting in ourselves and the spirit within. Trusting in the momentum we've created. We believe giving is its own reward. This perspective shift has allowed the flow of giving to cycle its way back. Instant karma is real whether you believe it or not.

This homeless journey all began with a wish-granting driving tour from Montreal to Miami, Miami to Los Angeles, and Los Angeles to Vancouver—with about forty stops inbetween. Soon after, we created the I Am Genie Foundation, followed by an egotistical desire to bring peace on earth before settling into being content with inner peace. Reminding me now of Rumi's quote, "Yesterday I was clever, so I wanted to change the world. Today I am wise, so I am changing myself." Small wish grant days soon became wish grant weeks, and what we were doing began to attract the attention of some people involved in TV. Then came our events with spiritual leaders Dr. Wayne Dyer, Deepak Chopra, Jack Canfield, Gabrielle Bernstein, James Van Praagh, Marianne Williamson, and most recently Eckhart Tolle. We evolved. Happiness quickened by living moment to moment.

Has it made us stronger? Yes. Have we followed our dreams? Totally. Would I change a thing? Nope. Because everything we've done has led us here, to this book. I give you this true story in hopes you find yours. I believe Oscar Wilde's words, "To live is the rarest thing in the world. Most people exist, that is all." Let's be rare together and remember Dr. Seuss's advice: "Don't cry because it's over; smile because it happened." Let's begin making that smile of yours a little wider.

Why read this book?

I'm not perfect. Nor am I your guru. That space is reserved for you. I've screwed up too many times to remember. My past is littered with incredibly bad decisions. In my twenties I lost my license for two years because of a drinking-and-driving accident, nearly killing my friends in the backseat—a higher power saving us all. I dislike doing anything too boring and get behind in accounting way more than is acceptable for the Canadian government. I even watch really bad reality TV and have a few drinks from time to time. Don't tell anyone, OK? In a nutshell, I'm an average dude who likes to live life on the edge, pushing myself to limits and experiencing things I would have never imagined. My scars are badges of honor, lest I forget. Leaving me with, well, a lot of lessons partially learned and experiences to share.

I know we all have secrets in our closets, the ones that make us feel fake or different. I've read all the books that give half a perspective. I want this to be whole. All me, all my understanding. All my love, passion, sadness, hate, inspiration, and glee. Inviting a connection.

I've spent the last seven years traveling in a magical world of the genie. Consciously following intuition. Something we all have, giving it many different names: Spirit. God. Good vibrations. Energy. Dreams. Doesn't really matter though, right? Because you know what I'm talking about. We all get it deep down. It's what the Chinese might refer to as the Tao. Saying that the Tao that can be named is not the Tao. That deep feeling of knowing you're going in the right direction, but even more than that. You are the right direction. A direct connection with source. No name needed or asked for. And we're not going to spend much time figuring that out here.

We can talk about spirituality till we're blue in the face (no pun intended). You can read all the books you want, memorizing all the right lines and saying all the right things. Playing copycat with other people's words and actions. But none of it matters until you experience you, feeling life's nature course through your veins. All the geographic boundaries, language barriers, and security checkpoints won't keep the imaginary boogeyman away. It doesn't matter. The grid will always be just the grid—a figment of our limitations. Not real in any true sense in a quantum reality. Just a fabricated fancy fence.

If your wish is escaping the rat race, traveling the world, being a superhero, changing jobs, or simply being more content with your life as it is, this book will help make it a reality—now, as opposed to a far-off place in the future that only exists in your mind. A neverland that may never happen. My experiences have taught me what your thoughts have attempted to cloud. Until now. Life doesn't have to be so hard. It really doesn't. Like looking for the gold at the end of the rainbow, you will find that the chase is an illusion. Everything you've ever needed, everything you've ever wanted, is within.

I began to notice something was seriously wrong with my life one day while on my way to work in Toronto soon after September 11, 2001. We were packed like sardines in a subway until the doors thankfully opened, prompting a mass of humans to shuffle their way to a tiny escalator leading to our cubicles and offices. For some reason on this particular day, I stopped and took a couple of steps back, watching everyone move together. It reminded me of rats winding their way toward cheese. Almost everyone looked as miserable as I was feeling. This wasn't living life. Only existing. And I was finished with existing. After about five minutes, the throng was gone, leaving me alone for a moment in an empty tunnel. I made the decision then and there to quit my job and start my own business. A make-it-count type of business I would later sell to look after my dad—planting the seed for a genie awakening.

When you ask most people what they want

or what will make them happy they, more often than not, answer with, "Loving family, nice house, great friends, and enough money to do whatever I want." That certainly wasn't my truth. I bought the first house I ever owned with cash. No mortgage, no debt, nothing. Barely thirty years old, great job, married with a beautiful son, another on the way. My brain told me I had arrived, that I was happy. The real me wasn't buying it. All I had really become was an ego wrapped in a family suit.

Aren't we all really chasing happiness by running on the hamster wheel? We've been told to equate happiness with money and "nice stuff," while most studies show that happiness decreases dramatically during your working years when you make the majority of your money and buy most of your nice stuff. There goes that theory.

Success, to me, is leaving nothing on the table. Giving it the best I've got. Being able to look at myself in the mirror before I go to sleep knowing, mistakes or not, I am being me. The results of my labor are simply guides that sometimes correlate with the work, sometimes not. The real test is within. Always reaching deeper and for higher versions of what I know I am but rarely achieve. Fleeting moments that, when actualized, make it all worthwhile.

Life isn't about keeping up with the Joneses or making it to the end with a bunch of articles of momentary pleasure. Whether or not you accomplish those shallow feats is neither here nor there. In fact, thinking in terms of future results is part of the problem–a striving strife, if you will. Now is all you have. It's all we'll ever have. Can you say you're doing your best with what you have right now? If not, why not? Be careful about stringing together too many "I wish this or that" or "somedays." There will be a someday that never gets its day. There may be a day, close to the end, when you sit on your deathbed and regret not following your dreams. And then what? Life is a beautiful, magical gift. Do yourself a favor: don't waste it on regrets and excuses.

If you are lost, finding your way back to your joy may not be easy. Because being yourself is so rare, most people don't understand it. The majority of your friends and family will likely disagree with you. Some may even try to stop you or block your path. You won't be acting like them anymore—a misunderstanding creating fear at first. You won't be going with the crowd. You'll begin to seem strange and foreign. They may even think you're losing it. I've been there; I know. However, my proposition to you is simple—read this tiny book of magic, understand life's great illusions, and follow the tips at the end of each chapter. If you are open, ready, and willing, it'll help you connect with your true self—the only place you'll ever find what you're looking for.

Truth begins and ends with you. The fact that you have this book in your hands means, on some level, you know the one and only simple truth: you and me, along with everything and everyone, are one perfect expanding and contracting energetic wavelike being. Too trippy for you? Get over it. It's always been this way. And, believe it or not, it may not be your destiny to sit behind a desk most of the time. Instead, wouldn't it be amazing to express who you truly are?

Don't you want to stop pretending? This book will urge you to listen to the hairs standing up on the back of your neck the next time they rise. Life is simplistically silly this way. And if you don't believe me, maybe Albert Einstein, the genius of our time, might convince you when he says, "The only real valuable thing is intuition." With words like these, I hope to serve and inspire, helping you find your magical lamp.

During a wish grant in Las Vegas with the Stupid Cancer charity years ago, I had the pleasure of bringing four people fighting cancer to meet Criss Angel, one of the world's leading magicians. The illusions he created were mind-altering and incredible. I simply couldn't understand how he did them. Leading me to wonder—why are our senses so misleading?

What came to me was this: the magic of life is disguised by a thin veil of culturally and historically created illusions. A story on top of reality, if you will. And to truly understand how to live a magical life, you must first understand what's real and what is not.

These past years have exposed me to the secrets to living a dream life. Many of the world's greatest spiritual teachers have taught me the secret tactics and perspectives I'm about to share with you now. Names that include Eckhart Tolle, Dr. Wayne Dyer, Deepak Chopra, Marianne Williamson, and Jack Canfield—and a few names you may not have heard of before like Gayle (my mom) and Bill (my dad) and many other beautiful truth-tellers I've met along the way.

Fulfilling all your deepest desires is much closer than you think if you begin to understand life's seven great illusions, which I'll share with you shortly. With this understanding, you can begin to see reality–not the made-up story in your head that your senses have a tendency to cloud–inviting the manifestation of your greatest wishes and your dream life.

1

THE ILLUSION OF DEATH

The first of life's great illusions says death is the end of life. Seeing through this veil, you come to realize a deeper understanding of death is required to truly understand life. Opposites of the same whole, death is life's greatest teacher and life is death's greatest friend.

Each day is a little life: every waking and rising a little birth, every fresh morning a little youth, every going to rest and sleep a little death.

- Arthur Schopenhauer

Being told that my father had less than one year left to live broke me for a time. Dad, barely fifty, was my anchor and the glue that kept our family together. Four months crept by, feeling like years, as I helplessly watched my strong, funny, caring, charismatic father deteriorate to a shell of his former self. Mercifully, on March 11, 2006, Dad, while sleeping peacefully next to my sister Hollie, let go.

That same morning I was abruptly awoken with the dreadfully needed news. If you've ever watched someone close to you be eaten by disease, you'll understand what I mean when I say "needed." If not, count your blessings. The path to death isn't always pretty. After a frantic drive to his Toronto house in rush hour, I finally arrived. I remember sitting in the car in front of his driveway, fearing the next moments. My first experience seeing a dead person was imminent.

Everything slowed as I opened his front door and heavily made my way to his room. The nightmare was peaking, fear building with each step. Trying to prepare myself, I had imagined this scene before—mistakenly assuming a breakdown, crying on the edge of his bed. Instead, I was stopped in my tracks the moment I saw him. The room was cold. The body was no longer my father. I could feel it. I waited for the tears to stream, helping release the pain. Nothing. Slowly I walked over, touching his once-beautiful face. Cold. Like me. A numb nothingness far worse than any sadness. The occasional tear that rolled down my face seemed forced just to please everyone around me. I loved my father—this I knew. But showing it felt fake. Feeling like a ticking bomb with no timer, about to explode, I left the room, no longer feeling anything for this lifeless body. My dad was gone.

"Any man can be a father, but it takes someone special to be a dad." Only a year before, when my son Jack was born, Dad had given me a pillow with this Anne Geddes quote inscribed on the front. When it became a remembrance, I felt cheated by love. I had not accepted reality, and my rage bubbled beneath the surface at Dad's funeral. In midst of the service, on my knees, eyes closed, listening to a reading, I don't remember what. I was in pain—exhaustingly so—actually making an effort to shed a tear. Again, nothing. Dead inside. A man with no feelings other than anger. Anger at the world. Anger at my father for leaving me.

Then it came. Out of the blue. Feeling it first in back of my heart. Energy tingled and sizzled through my body, filling it up. It was my father, but more, letting me know everything was OK. Waking me up. I cried, tears finally streaming down my face. Yet I wasn't strictly sad, feeling every emotion I'd ever felt, then more. Almost too much, but somehow perfect, and I was at peace for an infinite moment. Was it Dad saying good-bye? No. More like a hello. Our first spiritual greeting, consciously connecting us forever, pointing to a reality I had missed for so long. My father didn't die. None of us do.

"You're a ghost driving a meat-coated skeleton made from stardust." This anonymous quote pretty much sums it up. Standing on the front step of Dad's house on a crisp March day, looking at the big blue dumpster and the people we'd hired to help us clean house after his death, I remember thinking there must be more to it than all this stuff. My life felt like some big cosmic joke, a part in which I was now beginning to finally, consciously, play a role. As I watched Dad's possessions landing in the dumpster, one by one, a shift began.

The myth of death, for me, was continuing to show its true colors. The experiences associated with Dad's passing were teaching me that we live in a world filled with programmed thinking and stories that, when held to the light, fail to endure. We have the myths of security, control, geographic boundaries, culture, money, religion, stability, and even time. All concepts created by us to make us feel better about our imaginary selves.

Yet there was another perspective I hadn't realized for a long time. Programmed out of me, the truth began rushing back. As a young boy playing in the park, I remembered talking about how maybe we're all inside a giant without realizing it. Of course that couldn't be true, my friends and I agreed. But when we look squarely at this idea, it seems to be the case. The human race is an infinitely small piece of this giant universe we inhabit. Just take a look at any map of the universe with an arrow pointing to Earth. You can barely see it. And guess who you can barely see on Earth? You and me, making us and everything else in the universe pieces of a giant, ever-expanding, breathing organism. As my child-self liked to think, our individuality is simply an expression of this giant, much like the hair on our heads is an expression of our body. Alan Watts phrases it another way: "The individual may be understood neither as an isolated person nor as an expendable, humanoid working-machine. He may be seen, instead, as one particular focal point at which the whole universe expresses itself—as an incarnation of the Self, of the Godhead, or whatever one may choose to call IT," making us an experience or verb, instead of the static noun we imagine.

If you were to listen to science's definition of who you are, you might be surprised to hear you're a bit of a space cadet. Your body comprises approximately 7,000,000,000,000,000,000,000 ,000,000 atoms, and atoms are 99.999 percent space. Meaning, you are essentially space. Your five senses and learned notions mislead you into thinking you are your face, hands, hair, legs, skin, and everything else you see peering back at you in the mirror each morning. But, in fact, you are not. This vision, much like a dream, is really nothing more than a chemical reaction in your brain. You are a light, or more accurately, energy, surrounded by space. It's a simple, indisputable, freeing truth. The more you connect with this reality, the closer you come to understanding your true nature as an energetic being.

In his death, my father had succeeded in providing me with the most important lesson of my life. His spirit had provided a gateway to the universal consciousness where the illusion of separation dissolved into blissful awareness merging into the spirit of all creation. I had more than seen it; I felt the universe within and without, encompassing and surrounding my being where everything merged into bliss—a fleeting, anchoring moment that seemed to last forever, spurring a guided search for more of the same. That moment's beautiful fragrance lingers deep within my soul, even as I write this.

"I am Josh" might be the first example of me professing my ego. Walking into nonsense. In fact, most kids don't even understand being given a name, and refer to themselves in the third person early on. "Josh wants to eat" and "Josh wants to play" were probably my first sentences. I had not come to be controlled by my mind yet.

But very quickly and via conditioning, the

ego begins to control your life, and soon "I" and "my" creep in. "Don't touch my toy." "I want some juice!" "I'm going to my room!" At this point the ego is in control, disconnecting you on some level from everyone else. It's applauded in our society to be an individual, to stand out from the crowd, further strengthening our ego. But we unfortunately get it wrong. Because in the creation of our ego, we've disconnected ourselves from the most important thing—ourselves. Our true spirit selves. And the juxtaposition is that in our quest to be an individual, we've all become very similar—selfishly making ourselves number one, always maintaining and strengthening our fictional characters. Creating and reinforcing a story. Now is the time to see past this foolishness and create a new story, one that serves both you and our entire world. One that understands our true high-flying, wonderful, beautiful nature.

How can you see through the illusion of death? One way is through the practice of stillness and meditation. The fluid, space-filled nothingness that we all come from and return to. Like falling asleep while awake, meditation can lift the dark veil of death, showing true glory. "Be still and know I am God," one of the most popular quotes of all time, points to a very real truth.

The still, unchanging, free space is who we truly are and we need not die to go back there. We're actually always there, something our attachment to our incessant thoughts clouds most of the time.

To get ourselves back to this state we need to begin to distance ourselves from the problem, our thoughts. And one of the most effective ways to connect is via the very thing that keeps us alive— our magical breath. It is the invisible energetic force that powers us through our day, mostly without notice. And so is it with spirit. We rarely notice the infinite, constant, invisible presence within us, within our breath, until we most need it. It is usually only then, when we need it, that we praise it when it's received. We're a funny group in this way. Only appreciating something when it may be ripped away from us. Wanting it more than ever in that moment. But is your breath any less important right now as you read these words? Does it not facilitate the same life within you? Should you not praise it and show appreciation for it in this moment? Could you be conscious of it at all times, every day? Imagine such a world, full of appreciation in all moments for something as simple and as powerful as the very thing that gives you life. The Dalai Lama says, "If every eight-year-old in the world is taught meditation, we will eliminate violence from the world within one generation." Something you can come to appreciate with a daily meditation practice.

With your eyes closed, focusing on your breath, begin to notice your thoughts. Watch for them like a cat watching for a mouse to leave its hole, or as you might watch cars on a street below you while in a hot air balloon. Don't judge; just watch. What you might notice is that the thoughts eventually disappear altogether, even the one monitoring your breath, eventually merging with the infinite bliss of space and its universal connecting qualities. You may begin to notice blissful, wavelike feelings showering your being like a living, breathing, energetic force. You may even become aware that you are this breath. You are this bliss. You are this space. Pure, free, forever.

If you are looking for a particularly interesting meditation, I'd start with a wonderful Alan Watts death meditation. Start by thinking about his words, "Try to imagine what it will be like to go to sleep and never wake up-now try to imagine what it was like to wake up having never gone to sleep." This thought should bring you to the realization that death is simply a rebirth, as the universe abhors a vacuum. You can place yourself in that space between life and death at any moment. As you contemplate and imagine bringing yourself to this space now, begin to focus on your breathing with the incantation, "I Am that I Am; I Am that I Am." Slowing work your way to repeating, "I Am." Say these words over and over with a concentration on your breath until you again merge with your true self.

Another way to see through the illusion of death is to start relating to the reality of who you are: an energetic force. A decision maker connected to infinite possibilities. Ever feel as though you're holding back? Like there's something just below the surface waiting to break out and express itself? But you hold it back for fear of its beautiful, disruptive power. Byron Katie likes to say, "If you realized how beautiful you are, you would fall at your own feet." We are all shining lights, dimmed with mirrored conditioning. The thoughts that surround you as you look in the mirror when you wake up aren't the real you and never will be. They are just as much an illusion as the reflection you see staring back at you.

So, how do you break out of this mirrored conditioning? As the gateway to your soul, your eyes hold the key to the real you. With this in mind, I'll urge you try something very important anytime you look in the mirror today. Try not to look at that blemish on your face, or the few hairs that may be out of place. Try not to judge the illusion peering back at you. Right now you may be looking into the mirror forgetting how truly beautiful you are. Please don't do that. Don't listen to the "I'm not good enough" excuses. They don't serve you or anyone else. If you're in a funk reflecting a negative illusion, thinking everyone else is Snow White, use it as a cue to stop believing the negative hype your mind has created. Shatter the glass. Release yourself. Try to forget every ugly act you may have experienced or been a part of until this moment. The past is the past. This is now.

We don't always see our true selves when we look in the mirror, do we? We sometimes don't see love at all. Our fear, insecurity, and lack of acceptance reflect negativity back our way. I assume everyone has days like this. When we do this, we hold ourselves prisoner to that reflection, whether it be good or bad. It might serve you today and enslave you tomorrow. Marianne Williamson has a famous quote that says, "Your playing small does not serve the world. There is nothing enlightened about shrinking so that other people will not feel insecure around you. We are all meant to shine, as children do. We were born to make manifest the glory of God that is within us. It is not just in some of us; it is in everyone and as we let our own light shine, we unconsciously give others permission to do the same. As we are liberated from our own fear, our presence automatically liberates others."

Look deep into your eyes. Don't be afraid. Stare into the light. Stare into the depths of a universe peering back at you. Take off your mask. See the true you staring back. If you can honestly accomplish this feat, I'll promise one thing. You'll open a portal to your true power, bowing before its magnificent beauty. Remember the timeless beauty of who you really are. Something no mirror will ever be able to capture. Then start acting like it.

Begin to accept this reality by creating the character of your highest self. Dress like it, act like it, be that person for an entire day. The limiting idea of "you" is in itself a fictional character and, with practice you can create and mold one that best serves your natural tendencies. Treat life as a play where you are the director, actor, and producer. Assume everything you know is wrong.

Or, at the very least, only partially right. Forget everything you've been taught. Not so easy, is it? Just pretend. Spend one day doing it. Pretend you know nothing. When you look at anything for the entire day, try to forget that you know the thing's name or its function. When you meet someone new, treat them as though you have just seen another human (other than yourself) for the first time. Intrigue yourself with the magic that abounds all around you. Give yourself this gift and make yourself like an infant for one day.

Observing what you say after the words "I am" can also transcend the illusion of death. I am out of shape. I am tired. I am sick. Thoughts that may run through our heads, if we're not watching ourselves. The more we repeat them, the worse they get. Eventually, the chatter can't stay in our brains. It needs to get out. The thoughts become words and are shared. Now other people start believing, too. Building up steam, getting stronger with every utterance. Until finally we're exhausted.

I sometimes like to eat a little more than usual, developing a nice little Buddha belly. While alone poking and examining my new little paunch, I sometimes comment to myself, "I am fat." Every time I go down this rabbit hole, I catch myself and turn the sentence around, removing the negative. "I am strong and will go to the gym. I will change my eating habits." Feeling better already. My belly looks a bit smaller, too. The words you choose after "I am" are very powerful. Might as well use them wisely.

To see through the illusion of death, do the following:

- Meditate. Begin to create some space between yourself and your thoughts. Find the gap.

- Create a new character for yourself to be. One that is in line with your higher self. Practice seeing yourself with new eyes, lifting the perspective as a decision maker of infinite possibilities.

- Begin to notice what you say after the words "I am."

2

THE ILLUSION OF FORCE

The second of life's great illusions says that using force can provide value to you. The truth is, it is only through giving that you truly receive.

I slept and I dreamed that life is all joy. I woke and I saw that life is all service. I served and I saw that service is joy.

- Kahlil Gibran

"The love expressed today will last forever. It will follow me when I die as a bond we can all share," said my passenger.

I was driving down the highway toward Toronto with the top down on the convertible. Everyone was looking at the slick red car with what looked like a lady along with a blue man occupying the seats. Heads turned as we passed. My passenger was a beautiful woman in the final stages of her battle with cancer. It was chilly even for me with my mask on. Nevertheless, she asked me to put the top down to feel the wind through her thinned hair. This would be her first and last drive in a convertible. She knew it. Her husband and children were following in a van behind and in her weakened state she was pushing through this dream day for them. For love. Her comment expressing how love lasts forever is something I haven't forgotten, and never will.

Before her words, I didn't fully grasp the impact of what we were doing with our genie project. My primary goal was to take people away from their pain, giving them a bit of fun for a day. But her comment floored me. Would she really take this memory with her? Would it connect us all after she passed?

My father's passing had helped me begin to understand the words from the Song of Solomon: "Set me like a seal upon thy heart, love is as strong as death." But in this loving moment, with someone who had been a stranger only thirty minutes before, I came to fully comprehend that giving, in love, truly does pass all bounds. If you're looking for proof, imagine a beautiful moment shared with a loved one who has passed. It instantly connects you. Maya Angelou's famous quote really says it all: "I've learned that people will forget what you said, people will forget what you did, but people will never forget how you made them feel." And when you give of yourself to another, it makes both them and you feel good. Connecting you. This positive energy that you've put out into the universe goes around, gathers speed, and comes back to you stronger than ever. Like a love boomerang.

It's not so much that I like helping people, in and of itself, that spurs me to grant wishes. There's more to it than that. The primary motivation is more selfish. It comes from the feeling I receive. It's deeper and more robust than the simple actions, although they go hand in hand. A mysterious connection is established when you help someone. A release of pressure, for both you and them. A beautiful freedom or expansion that takes place. A strengthening.

This may be the reason why helping, even without recognition, can feel so powerful. In this, you are placing the totality of your awareness on that feeling inside. Nothing is being wasted on the result or recognition you will receive. That feeling inside is, for lack of a better word, God. An all-encompassing energy connecting us. I have come to believe our primary reason for being, in its deepest form, is to connect with this energy and carry out its wishes.

Force, on the other hand, may work for a time. People may be nice to your face, for fear of repercussions, while talking quietly behind your back. But as history has proven time and again through every single one of the world's dictators, they eventually fall from their lofty perches. Take Hitler, Stalin, Gadhafi, and Saddam Hussein, to name a few. Force dies, love and giving survives, for one simple reason—force is an illusionary state with a very limited illusionary lifespan.

How can you see through the illusion of force? The first way is to enter into a state of giving. Set an alarm on your phone that says, "How many people will I serve today?" I do. It reminds me as soon as I wake up to be thankful and express my true nature as a gift to the world. Then immediately after your meditation, actively look to do something for someone else. It need not be a big wish grant or something that costs money. It could be cooking breakfast for your wife and family or going on Facebook and paying someone a compliment. Another great option is giving people twenty-second hugs. Ingrid and I do this every morning we see each other and it's a fantastic way to start your day. Above all else, keep it simple and practice doing what your intuition tells you to do.

The second way to master the illusion of force is to silently wish everyone you see well-being. Connect with their eyes as you do it. In essence, pray for them. The wonderful thing you may notice right away is how little you normally notice people as they pass you. This turns the tables on that practice by acknowledging their existence as you silently wish them well. Creating a "namaste" effect. Again, connecting you to others.

Another great way to transcend the illusion of force is to practice receiving. Never look a gift horse in the mouth. Giving and receiving should be balanced; to not accept gifts throws off this balance. When someone pays you compliment, take it. Believe it. When someone wants to buy you dinner, say thanks and eat up. This is something a lot of givers have trouble with. If you can relate to this challenge, understand that giving and receiving are two sides of a whole and that disregarding one will cut off the current or flow of energy.

This is something I struggled with in my spiritual walk early on. People would literally bend over backward to offer me money while on dream days and I'd never accept it. Then one day, having just finished a wish grant in Jacksonville, Florida, making my way back to my hotel room, with my mask off and blue eye makeup and red suit still on, someone stopped me right outside my room. They had just seen us on the nightly news and wanted to give me $50 to help with everything we were doing. This had happened many times before, and I would always refuse. I was just about to make the same mistake when something inside me said, "Accept it." It was a small act, but from that moment on I began to receive more and more. Until that moment, the genie was always one step away from pending failure, with barely enough to make ends meet.

I hope this story acts as a funny reminder, next time you forget to receive:

It was flooding in California. As the flood waters rose, a man was on the stoop of his house and another man in a rowboat came by. The man in the rowboat told the man on the stoop to get in and he'd save him. The man on the stoop said no—he had faith in God and would wait for God to save him.

The flood waters kept rising and the man had to go to the second floor of his house. A man in a motor boat came by and told the man in the house to get in because he had come to rescue him. The man in the house said, "No thank you." He had perfect faith in God and would wait for God to save him.

The flood waters kept rising. Pretty soon they were up to the man's roof and he got out on the roof. A helicopter came by, and the pilot lowered a rope and shouted down to the man in the house to climb up the rope because the helicopter had come to rescue him. The man in the house wouldn't get in. He told the pilot that he had faith in God and would wait for God to rescue him.

The flood waters kept rising and the man in the house drowned. When he got to heaven, he asked God where he'd gone wrong. He told God that he had perfect faith in him, but God had let him drown.

"I sent you two boats and a helicopter," said God. "What more do you want from me?"

To see through the illusion of force, do the following:

- Enter into a state of giving the moment you wake up. Put an alarm on your phone that says, "How many people will I serve today?" Immediately after waking up, meditate and then do one thing that will help someone out. It need not be a big gesture. A simple smile or hug could be enough to change a person's life. Don't underestimate the power of your love.

- Silently wish everyone you see well-being.

- Practice receiving. Only giving is an unbalanced relationship sure to crack. If you don't tend to both aspects of these complimentary activities, the currency of life will become stagnant and broken.

3

THE ILLUSION
OF SECRECY

The third of life's great illusions says there
are secrets. In reality, the universe is always
watching and listening, and every thought,
every action, produces a reaction.

When given the choice between being right and being kind, choose kind.

- Dr. Wayne Dyer

For me, meeting Dr. Wayne Dyer for the first time was kind of like meeting Jesus. I know that sounds weird, but his books had a deep spiritual effect on me. And when you meet Jesus, you need to make sure your hair is looking good. Well, that's what I did anyway, rushing to the bathroom in the airport to fix a mess the Newfoundland wind had created. Reading his books had connected me and millions of others through the words of spirit that came through him. I wouldn't go so far as to say I idolized this man, but I was super excited to meet him. More than anything, I wanted to learn what made him tick. Understand more. Simply be in his presence. I hoped he wasn't an asshole. I hoped he was the person he portrayed in his books. I hoped he was real.

Waiting with Ingrid at the bottom of the tiny airport escalator as everyone on his flight passed one by one, I began to get nervous. What if he didn't like me? What if he wasn't on the flight? What if he decided to not come? I knew he had been having back issues recently. I hoped for the best, but my worries were getting the best of me. It was taking too long. The last of the people had deplaned and still no Wayne. Another five minutes. Still no Wayne. Then, out of the blue, he and his beautiful daughter Skye appeared. One of his fans was talking to him. In an instant all the worries disappeared. I knew we would be friends. I knew he wasn't an asshole. I knew he would be real. Within moments we greeted each other with a bear hug. The beginning of a great friendship.

His presence was the first thing I noticed— always fully there and aware. Being in his company made me happy. Not regular grown-up happy. Being-a-kid happy. Giggly happy. He hung on my every word with genuine interest. I could feel it. Something I would watch him do many times with many people in the upcoming days. Giving in every moment. On the flip side, when he spoke, everyone listened. The self-assured, kind, intelligent pace of his tone drew you in.

On the drive to the hotel we got to know each other a bit better. It was spring, running into summer (for Newfoundland), and the flowers were in full bloom—something I didn't really notice at first, being too busy with the upcoming event. But the beauty wasn't lost on Wayne. He was mesmerized by it, commenting on it during the entire drive. It made me take notice. Yes, it was beautiful, extraordinarily so now. How had I missed that? "Mental note: be more conscious," I thought to myself. We arrived at Monastery Spa and Suites, and right outside the entrance was a huge lilac tree, almost hitting Wayne as he opened the door of the Escalade. When Wayne gets excited his voice goes up a couple of octaves. It's endearing and happens a lot. When he saw the tree, he took one of the branches and began to take in its essence with deep, deep inhalations. He was in heaven. I could see how it powered him up, being at one with nature.

After Wayne and Skye checked in and freshened up a bit, we met in the lobby and went out for lunch to a café in a museum called The Rooms. A spectacular spot overlooking St. John's Harbor and the Atlantic Ocean pointing toward Europe. We were hoping for a spot, but it's usually quite busy, and this day was no exception. The attendant told us it would be about a twenty-minute wait, so we decided to try to find another place. Just before we started walking away, I noticed my cousin Desiree, who had lived with us for a couple of years when we were growing up, seated by the window with her family, including my supercute goddaughter, Ava. I mentioned this to Wayne just before we reached the elevator and he asked me, "Why didn't you go over and say hi?" I said I didn't want to make him wait. He was having none of that. "We have to go back," he said. "I would love to meet them." After a quick introduction, Wayne had them laughing as he balanced a spoon on his nose, playing with my goddaughter. A few moments later, a table opened up. Wayne's response: "See what happens when you follow your intuition?"

Wayne's actions during our six days together would continue to remind me of someone with a deep understanding that the universe truly was listening to our every thought and action. Watching him go about his day was inspiring on a level I have rarely experienced before or since. One of those incredible people who make you want to be a better person, his commitment to self-actualization was without compare. Quite out of the blue, while driving down Water Street on our way home from lunch, an intuitive message came to him.

We had just passed Trixie, an iconic local St. John's personality, who has since passed. Her sometimes revealing sense of style and dyed blond hair were two of her many unique traits. Driving slowly down the road because of traffic, Ingrid began sharing a lovely experience she'd had with Trixie. One evening, while out with friends, a feeling came over her to cross the street and give this woman a hug. When she did, Trixie began crying. A healing connection initiated by Ingrid following her inner guidance.

"Stop the car!" Wayne's voice rose a little to let me know he was serious. After parking next to the curb, he jumped out and walked down the street, stopping in front of Trixie. "God put the desire in my heart to give this to you. God bless you." Wayne handed her all the money in his pocket and walked back to the car. After settling back into the seat, Wayne looked at me saying, "When desire matches an idea, you listen."

Wayne didn't stop here with his mindfulness. It was part of everything he did, including what he put in his body and how he treated it. Every morning without fail we'd both go for a ninety-minute swim, and he practiced a strict vegetarian, no-alcohol, gluten-free lifestyle. He was even, believe it or not, a conscious music listener. When he bought myself, Ingrid, and her mom tickets to a Sting concert so his daughter Skye could see one of her favorite acts perform, I noticed he listened to the words very intently before moving to the beat.

"Good morning, this is God. I will be handling all of your problems today. I will not need your help, so have a miraculous day." This Wayne Dyer quote assumes God is in control. And if you believe that, you need only concern yourself with understanding that God is always talking to you, pointing you in the right direction. And with conscious listening, you will never be led astray. Some of us just need to remember how to listen again. The universe doesn't need our help figuring it out; she just wants a dance partner to fulfill the experience.

How can you see through the illusion of secrecy and begin to make more conscious decisions?

The universe has one simple wish: it wants to experience itself through you. Begin to imagine you're constantly being watched by the universe. It wants your desires to come true, because those desires are its own. Even the negative ones, because they have a part to play as well. Pain, the opposite of joy, forges us into stronger people, allowing us to see the light. So if you have a negative thought or worry, help it along its way. Same goes for positive thoughts. The wonderful thing is, you get to choose your thoughts. If you believe it's true for you, then it is.

Begin today the practice of watching your thoughts. Choose the ones that best serve you and the people around you. Your thoughts are the root cause of all the world's highs and lows. Everything in human creation starts with a thought. Before any action, ask yourself, "Is this decision based on love or fear?" If it's a fear-based decision, the consequences will not be for your evolution. If love is your intention, beautiful things obviously manifest.

The second way is to choose positivity no matter what happens. For an entire day, practice not reacting to anything you perceive as negative. At first you may notice it makes you feel small and weak. That's simply your ego talking. After a few moments of nonreaction, you'll notice your spirit expanding and, in essence, congratulating you. When you engage in negativity, it breeds more of the same. Give yourself time with this process and consciously take in everything someone says to you. Take a few deep breaths. Ask yourself, "Is anything that this person is saying true?" You may be surprised at your answer if you can look at it objectively. With practice you will. Sit with it and see how it makes you feel. Try to remember all the times when someone has said or done something to really piss you off, where you've instantly reacted only to regret it later. Remember that conscious decision making doesn't reward ego gratification. Negative produces more negative and a bigger fire. You aren't what people do to you. You can always choose a positive frequency.

The final way is to be conscious of what you put in your body and the people you surround yourself with. Study upon study says what you put in your body affects your mood, and can even be linked to mental disorders that cause you to lose your ability to control your reactions to external stimuli. It's not hard for us to understand that we are what we eat. Before his passing, Dr. Wayne Dyer was very conscious of this fact. And I know there are a lot of complicated theories on how to eat healthfully, but it's relatively simple to eat a balanced diet that will keep your body regulated. The diet I've always followed includes eating as much protein as possible via nonanimal sources, a lot of beans, and as many vegetables as possible. Try to avoid carbohydrates except within one and one-half hours of doing a strenuous activity. Sweat every day. Treating your body need not be a complicated feat. Eat real foods and exercise.

Same goes for the people you choose to associate yourself with most. Their thoughts and actions have an effect on you both consciously and subconsciously. Motivational teacher Jim Rohn said, "You are the average of the five people you spend the most time with." Take a look at your top five and you'll notice you likely share a lot of characteristics. If you feel your true character isn't shining through as it should, it might be a sign to get new friends. This is a very normal phase of any spiritual transformation and can lead to sadness and feelings of nostalgia. The key is to not judge your friends, but rather to become aware that they may not be helping you evolve and grow. Remember that all the magic happens outside your comfort zone, and beginning to spend time with people that are more aligned with you right now may be the greatest gift you can give to yourself and the people around you. If your friends are true, they may come to meet you on your journey.

To see through the illusion of secrecy, do the following:

- Begin to imagine that you're constantly being watched by the universe.

- Choose to maintain a positive frequency.

- Be conscious of what you put in your body and the people you surround yourself with. You are the average of the top five people you hang out with the most.

4

THE ILLUSION
OF HARDSHIP

The fourth of life's great illusions states
that life is hard. The truth is, you just make
it that way. There are no problems, only
challenges. Begin to understand the 20
percent of your efforts that produce 80
percent of the positive results, and your life
begins to take on a wonderful flow.

Pareto's Law can be summarized as follows: 80% of the outputs result from 20% of the inputs.

- Timothy Ferriss

Today, I believe life is simple. Bruce Lee adds to this truthful chorus by saying, "It is not a daily increase, but a daily decrease. Hack away at the inessentials." We tend to make life complicated with our habitually repetitive thought patterns, much of which are completely unnecessary. I'd like to propose a truth you may have missed: we really only have two states, "busy" and "free." Our busyness leads to wars, stress, unease, and an overall feeling of overwhelmed unhappiness. Yet we continue on this path because, for most of us, it's all we know. We've become experts occupying ourselves doing what we don't like doing.

Jack Canfield, co-creator of the Chicken Soup for the Soul series of books, is one of the best-selling authors of all time. He's also one of the first people who mentored Tim Ferris, the man who brought the concept of the Pareto principle back to the masses, with his hugely successful The 4-Hour Workweek blockbuster book we'll get to in a moment.

What you may not know about Jack is that he kissed a codfish onstage with me in St. John's, Newfoundland. This strange tradition performed on non-Newfoundlanders involves having a shot of a rather nasty-tasting rum called Screech along with a short recitation and the kissing of a cod. The purpose is to make them honorary Newfoundlanders. Jack did it for the experience, certainly not taking himself too seriously. Perfectly genuine in every way, he reminded me of one of those people that everyone just loves. In the three days we spent together, he was always the same nice, caring, interesting guy with a sense of self-assurance that you rarely to see in others. He knew who he was, told the truth always, and really did not care what anyone else thought of him. His guidance came from within—the kind of person who thought, "What others think about you is none of your business." One of his more famous quotes, and a wonderful teaching that he gifted me.

When I first started sharing my writings on Facebook, I imagined that past friends of mine would think I'd lost it. Being around Jack helped me get past this limiting habit that makes so many of us feel tethered. Helping unlock one of the illusionary chains of hardship. Now when I feel like posting something on Facebook, I do it as long as I think it may help another, not caring if I get ridiculed or made fun of. And you know what? The sky hasn't fallen yet. The world has continued on its path, and best of all, you're reading this book.

It's not surprising that Jack Canfield was one of the mentors that helped Tim Ferris with his 4-Hour Work Week success, because he understood the Pareto principle or the "eighty-twenty rule" better than most. He understood that to be successful, you need to concentrate on the 20 percent of your activities that are most important. Your dreams. While sitting in the Newfoundland television control room watching Jack Canfield give a promotional interview for an event with Meetings with Remarkable People host and dear friend Jesse Stirling, I was struck by something he said. Jack mentioned that he always carried a card listing his dreams with him and would review it every day to ensure he was on the right track. A key aspect of the consistent focus needed to bring your dreams to reality. Jack understood that to fulfill your dreams, focus was key. Taking responsibility for his actions with this daily reminder of what was truly important to him. For most, it's all too easy to get lost in the hamster wheel of activity for the sake of activity. Forgetting your "why."

How can you see through the illusion of hardship? The first way is to begin to understand which aspects of your life are creating happiness. For most people, these activities are the ones that are most productive and constitute 20 percent or less of their time. To understand what your 20 percent is, an objective appraisal of where you stand today is needed, while being careful to stay away from excuse-laden rationalizations for why your life is so hard. Your hard life only means one thing—you need to start making some hard choices. Here and now we begin following Rumi's advice to "be like the tree and let the dead leaves drop." You and I have been holding onto things that don't serve us for too long, reminding me now of a wonderful Buddhist parable.

Once two traveling monks arrived at a river. There they discovered a woman struggling to get across. Without a second thought, the older of the two monks asked the woman if she needed help, then swiftly picked her up and carried her across to the other bank.

It should be understood that for monks, especially in ancient times, any contact with the opposite sex would be strongly frowned upon, if not forbidden. The actions of the older monk greatly troubled the younger monk, who allowed his feelings to fester for several miles while they continued their journey.

Finally, the younger monk confronted the older monk. "How could you have done such a thing? We are not even supposed to be in a woman's presence, but you touched her, even carried her!"

The older monk calmly replied, "I put that woman down miles ago, back at the river. But you are still carrying her." The younger monk realized the older monk was indeed correct and they continued on their journey.

Antoine de Saint-Exupéry said, "Perfection is achieved, not when there is nothing more to add, but when there is nothing left to take away." Our aim here is to strive for perfection by doing less, stripping away anything that isn't alive and dynamic. If you look closely enough at your life, you may notice that the activities that are producing the lowest results are most likely causing you the greatest problems. Tim Ferris, the first person to highlight this in my life, summarizes it beautifully with this quote: "When I'm really feeling overwhelmed, I actually focus on the negative, which is a good thing. I focus on eliminating as much as possible before I focus on doing more. What can I get rid of? What are the psychic anchors, which are tethering me to the ground where I'm trying to sprint forward, but I'm just dragging this weight behind me. I focus on a massive elimination first. I try to remove as much as possible so that I have fewer moving pieces to think about. So elimination is a huge part of why I get anything done."

What you'll find is that story you tell yourself is littered with excuses that, with time, become regrets, and life flashes before your eyes before you have time to blink. A ground-breaking objective analysis of your activities is needed. Specifically, let's focus on the things most likely weighing you down and prune your tree of life. Freeing you to grow into your full potential.

Take a look at an average day of yours. Map

it out, detailing everything you do. Now list the top activities that produce the most positive results. Also list the top activities that produce the most negative results. This isn't rocket science here, folks; we're just performing an eighty-twenty analysis and attempting to decrease the 80 percent of your activities that produce little or no benefit to you. We're cutting the fat. Once you have your list, create a "to do" list and a "not to do" list. Like my mom always says, "You need to know what you are not good at." If you can, eliminate any activities on the "not to do" list immediately. Just do it. If not, start to think about ways you can change your life to make this happen. We don't want you to be tied down by things that don't serve you any longer than necessary. Now put more focus into your new "to do" list. Repeat monthly, weekly, daily, as needed.

If you're having trouble with this process, here's a little tip that will make your life drastically better right now. Eliminate all TV watching that is not inspirational. You may find this hard to believe, but the average man spends ten years watching TV while women come in at thirteen years! With it, you get bombarded with thoughts that are effectively being imprinted on you. Thoughts like: "I am out of shape." "I am tired." "I am sick." "I am going to be killed by a terrorist." Thoughts that may run through your head thousands of times a day. Do you eat fast food every day? Probably not. And if you do, you probably know the negative effects it can have. It's something you put in your body that causes health issues, lack of energy, weight increase—the list goes on. The same goes for the information you allow yourself to listen to. It literally influences the way you think, leading to changes in your emotional state and actions. And believe it or not, you are addicted to all the fast information out there. Let's prove it with a simple test. Put this book down and don't watch a TV, read a newspaper, go on the Internet, use a computer, or answer your phone for twenty-four hours. I can feel the tension building up in you as you even contemplate doing this. Does it feel like you need these things to survive? Don't you think an addict feels the same way about his or her drug or alcohol of choice? Don't you think they think they need it, too? Let's go cold turkey. Stop watching TV. Replace your TV habit with reading, meditating, hanging out with friends. Almost anything, really. If you can't do this, begin watching educational programs or shows with no commercials that inspire.

Another way to see through any hardships

is to listen to Jack Canfield and truly believe that what other people think of you is none of your business. Something the iconic Mahatma Gandhi realized with the quote, "I will not let anyone walk through my mind with their dirty feet." For the moment you are doing something to look good, find favor, impress a client, or any number of reasons you may want someone to think highly of you, you begin to listen to an external master. Have you ever attempted to listen to two people at the same time while they are talking to you? Not much fun, is it? Damn near impossible to hear what they're both saying. In much the same way, if you are directing your attention to what you think someone else is thinking of you, you are shutting out the only voice that matters—your intuition. As this story illustrates:

> A man goes to an outdoor market to buy food. He sees a stand with a sign overhead: FRESH FISH SOLD HERE TODAY.
>
> He says to the vendor, "Your sign is too long. You don't need all those words."
>
> "What do you mean?" asks the vendor.
>
> "Take down the word 'fresh'; people will know it's fresh at this outdoor market."

"OK," says the vendor, and he takes down FRESH.

"Now, about the word 'today,'" says the man. "When else?"

The vendor takes down TODAY. The sign now says FISH SOLD HERE.

"Here? Where else?" says the shopper.

The vendor takes down HERE, and the sign says, FISH SOLD.

"Sold. Do you think anyone thinks you are giving the fish away?"

The vendor takes down SOLD, and the sign now says FISH.

"Fish!" says the shopper. "With a smell like this, you need a sign?"

When I began to introduce the genie and my spiritual practice to every aspect of my life, it wasn't all milk and honey. I started realizing very quickly that some people would never see me as who I presently was. This new me, in their eyes, was fake, with the previous version of me being my true self. "You look like a blue devil." "You're just in it for yourself." "That mask is ugly and stupid." "Grow up." "He's full of it." Just a few of the comments in an average day of being a genie. The world is full of sometimes well-meaning yet mean people. By now, we realize that resistance is futile. Acceptance that we all have different perspectives is the key to happiness and freedom from hate. And therein lies the key love. Putting yourself in someone else's shoes. Attempting to understand their unique circumstances.

The final stage of releasing yourself from the imaginary chains of hardship involves practicing the art of "no defense." When people lash out, it's usually because they've been lashed. And everyone truly is doing the best they can with the information they have. I realize being compassionate to someone who is insulting you is not an easy task. Byron Katie says, "Defense is the first act of war." A lack of defense requires a very strong connection with your source when you feel anger bubbling. Staying calm and not reacting when someone is directing their anger at you requires practice.

Whenever anyone actively attacks me, I try to remember Lao Tzu's words, "Do you have the patience to wait till the mud settles and the water is clear? Can you remain unmoving till the right action arises by itself?" You and this world don't evolve with fighting; evolution happens with ideas and dreams. Wars end with the highest ideals of freedom and compassion. Next time you get mad, give yourself a time-out. Walk away from the situation. Do something completely different. Catch your breath. Don't react for at least an hour. You'll find that when you come back, the environment may have changed and you can discuss solutions, not problems. Or not. Either way, you will not have allowed another to have power over your actions. Remember Bernard Shaw's quote, "I learned long ago, never to wrestle with a pig. You get dirty, and besides, the pig likes it."

To see through the illusion of hardship, do the following:

- Become intimate with the 20 percent of your life that is creating 80 percent of your success and happiness. Then do more of that.

- Stop caring what others think of you.

- Give yourself the "no defense" challenge.

5

THE ILLUSION OF LIMITATIONS

The fifth of life's great illusions states that limitations are real. Truth is, we are newly born every minute, and our attachment to who we were yesterday can restrict us.

When you are inspired by some great purpose, some extraordinary project, all your thoughts break their bonds: your mind transcends limitations, your consciousness expands in every direction, and you find yourself in a new, great, and wonderful world. Dormant forces, faculties, and talents become alive, and you discover yourself to be a greater person by far than you ever dreamed yourself to be.

- Patanjali

The fifth of life's great illusions states that limitations are real. Truth is, we are newly born every minute, and our attachment to who we were yesterday can restrict us. Just look around you for the proof. All living things are in a constant cycle of expansion, with our hardships or challenges being our biggest opportunities for evolution and growth. If you develop the habit of doing two to three things each day that you can start and finish, your "impossible" will begin to become "probable" and eventually "actual."

Every society thinks they have it all figured out, surprising themselves when they unveil a new discovery. The world was flat. We couldn't fly. Another gigantic earth-like planet was supposedly impossible. Until it wasn't. Our five senses are misleading. Or at the very least, grossly out of touch with objective reality, providing us with such a limited view that they may actually serve as an obstacle to the truth. And science has already proven this. As Alan Watts likes to further illustrate, "The prevalent sensation of oneself as a separate ego enclosed in a bag of skin is a hallucination which accords neither with Western science nor with the experimental philosophy-religions of the East."

What to do if you can't find that big idea? What happens if you don't know what to do with your life? You can't exactly create a dream plan if you don't have a dream, right? This section invites you to stop listening to other people's voices and start listening to and acting on your own inner voice—that inner tingly feeling that fills you up with an unexplainable warmth and lets you know that an idea, vision, or dream experience you are about to undertake is the right thing to do. These feelings are your "God bumps" and they give you access to an inner knowing that, when trusted, will guide your life effortlessly.

When I look back on the first-ever

appearance of the genie, it makes me smile because, truth be told, no sane person would ever have done it the way we did it that day. I had stayed up much too late, watching TV.

It was 5:00 a.m. on a supercold, almost drizzly day in Calgary, Alberta. Something I wasn't expecting in the middle of July. It was still dark, feeling more like winter than the middle of summer. A reverse Chinook, I guess. I was standing next to the Breakfast TV morning news anchor counting down to broadcast to about a million people on live TV. The two cameras in front and an Enzo Ferrari behind blocked me in. No turning back or running away now. Dressed like a freaky-looking blue genie, my mind went blank for a moment as the gravity of the situation hit me. I realized during the countdown to going live that I had no idea what I was going to say. Added to this, we didn't even know who we were going to surprise with the dream day we planned. Just to make it more interesting (or frightening, depending on how you look at it), we'd decided to pull a random person off the street for this first wish grant. I certainly had no idea where this genie thing was going. There was zero business plan. Or any plan, for that matter.

Sometimes it really helps to wear a mask. I was frightened to death standing in front of those cameras for the first time. I remember thinking that maybe I was one of those people who had gone insane but just didn't know it yet. The even crazier thing was, I loved it! This was living as far as I was concerned. It had only been two months since I proclaimed I would dress up as a genie and grant wishes, and here I was. Doing it. Experiencing it. Feeling alive for the first time since I could remember. I didn't want to let this feeling go. The interview started off a little shakily, mostly because I could barely open my mouth with the new silicone mask clamping it shut pretty tightly. A new door in life's journey had opened. One that allowed me to express and experience my true self.

I began to understand Joseph Campbell's words, "Follow your bliss and the universe will open doors for you where there were only walls." It was exciting. Although I never could have envisaged that I would be granting wishes as a dude dressed as a blue genie. While none of it was making much sense to me or the people around me, it didn't matter. For the first time in my adult memory, I wasn't thinking so much. Instead, my heart was in the driver's seat. And things that couldn't be rationally explained began to happen. We were invited on CTV the next day, then back on Breakfast TV, and incredibly, we found the perfect person to surprise right there in the studio. After a fast-paced forty-eight hours of connecting with an amazing family, racing cars, scuba diving, and unadulterated luxury, I knew I had found my calling. This stranger-than-fiction story had begun.

After the genie inspiration came over me (while hungover) in my La-Z-Boy in Montreal, it would have been all too easy for me not to listen. I could have listened to someone else's voice. Followed the "get a job" plan. The one that said, "You're crazy, you're going to make a fool of yourself. What about your kids? How are you going to support them?" It would have been easy to go back to the way society wanted to see me. But I didn't. I had been listening to others for too long. At my breaking point, I was much too unhappy doing it their way. This vulnerability primed me for this true life experience. Because it felt like I had nothing to lose.

When you have a gut feeling, it's your responsibility to go with it. Follow it through. Logical reasoning will sometimes be driven by fear and move you away from your dreams—if you let it. Learn how to differentiate between your intuition and fear, then use this "clean" version of logic to follow through.

Inspirations are like beautiful passing ships in the night. Because they may never come back, an honoring of their splendor is appreciated by the universe. Wayne Dyer taught me that if the idea is matched with a strong desire to make it a reality, pay extra special attention. The moment the inspiration of the genie came, it then became my job to follow the directions of spirit, playing with it through testing and execution. This is actually what your mind was built for. It's almost like your heroic spirit says, "Do this. I want to experience what it feels like!" At this point, if you don't use your mind to get out of your chair and stop watching TV, eating chips, or searching the Internet, then the power from the inspiration and associated energy is clouded by your static mind, convincing you to follow the status quo. This way of being will bring you to a heavier, darker, lower frequency, or the ego side of the pendulum. Fortunately, I had reached a point where listening to my ego wasn't working for me anymore. The darkness had shown me the light.

Let's face it, becoming a genie definitely wasn't logical. And that's to be expected. Your intuition won't necessarily think in terms of logical cause and effect, because that's not its reality. Your spirit isn't localized or interested in following the norm. It wants an expansive expression. Excitement begging your thoughts for permission to be itself. Or as Wayne Dyer states, "If it excites you, the very presence of that inner excitement is all the evidence you need to remind you that you're aligned with your true essence." This excitement is how your spirit speaks to you. Dreams, inspirations, and desires are the language of the soul. Even the ones that may get you in trouble, for they have a lesson to teach in the grand scheme of things. Wayne Dyer goes even further on the subject, saying, "Any idea accompanied with desire is God talking to you."

Gautama Buddha says, "Your purpose in life is to find your purpose and give your whole heart and soul to it." And that about sums up life in one amazing reflection. Knowing that I'm a spirit having a human experience helps me realize that my primary purpose is to inspire others. It's the reason I'm writing this book and the reason why I travel around granting wishes and hosting events with inspirational speakers like Eckhart Tolle and

Deepak Chopra.

I love the quote by Anaïs Nin, "And the day came when the risk to remain tight in a bud was more painful than the risk it took to blossom." As a society, most of us have forgotten how to listen to our inner voices for fear of failing or not fitting in. But we have it backward. Bronnie Ware, a writer and songwriter from Australia who spent several years caring for dying people in their homes, wrote a book, The Top Five Regrets of Dying. When terminally ill people were questioned about any regrets they had or anything they would do differently, five common themes surfaced again and again. But the number-one regret, by a long shot, was: "I wish I'd had the courage to live a life true to myself, not the life others expected of me." I don't think anyone wants to die with their music left in them. Or end up on their deathbed saying, "What if my whole life has been wrong?"

I believe one of the biggest sources of anxiety can be traced to not following your dreams. These deepest of desires point to who you are, and not being true to them will cause all sorts of unhappiness to manifest. And if you follow your heart, I promise there will be people who resist. Don't let these dissenting opinions stop you. Go out and do just one thing today that will bring more happiness into your life. Do what you love while offering no excuses to yourself or anyone else. This is your life to live, and now is the time to begin.

Let's bring the magic back. Time to wake up and realize that most of us are wasting our lives doing things that we don't want to do and listening to people that don't know what they're talking about. We all have very unique reasons for existence that have been clouded by the static or rust on our line to the source. Here and now we clean the line and open you up to your genie within. You may have been sleepwalking, hoping someone else will give you the answer to your purpose. The truth is, no guru, master, business, religious leader, or anyone you put on a pedestal will have the ability to tell you what God is instructing you to do. They may be able to help you open up to the universal whisperings, as I am hopefully doing here, but that's about it.

Most people have been trained to think that other people know what's best for them. You've been conditioned to think this way, and almost everyone does it throughout their life in one way or another, in small and big decisions. I went to university and got a business degree because I thought that's what everyone wanted me to do, not because I had a burning desire within to do so. Do I regret it? No, it was part of my path and I honor it as a divine lesson. Would I do it again the same way, knowing what I know today? Of course not. We evolve and learn the lessons along the way.

Perceiving your dreams and burning desires as energetic gifts that initiate action may be something you don't have much practice with. Almost as soon as we are born, we are taught to repress our desires for the supposed greater good, from sometimes well-meaning people who think they know what's best for you. The problem is, they don't know what your function is on this earth—only your spirit does. Thinking they know the real you, or projecting what they think is best for you, they take a guess at what you need. But this is, at best, a watered-down version of your destiny, clouded by their personalities. In reality, your dreams and desires are personal to you. To access them, it's important you come from a place of stillness. That place of nothingness from which everything comes in your imagination. That peaceful space within you that never changes. That place called God.

A burning desire attached to an idea is God talking to you, and when you begin to repress this divination, unhappiness ensues. The aim here is to connect with your true desires, accepting these inspirational gifts without repression or judgement, exciting yourself to treat each day as a part of the exceptional life that it is. The aim is to continue your dreams in your waking hours, becoming one with love. As Dr. Seuss points out, "You know you're in love when you can't fall asleep because reality is finally better than your dreams." Let's become one with our dreams.

Let's bring you to your happy place by way of a process that will entail reworking the busy habits that have been programmed into you since you were first born. Most of what you do daily is done without your conscious awareness. In fact, 96 percent of what you do is done with your subconscious, and your ego is programmed into this. We will need to fix these bugs and reprogram you with new thoughts and actions. This section won't be about following the rules, filling out the right forms, going to the right school, or getting the right job. That's the ego side of things. This will be about following one thing—your burning desires. It will be about remembering what it is you truly love to do and filling your life with it.

Our first step together will entail helping you listen to the sweet whisperings of your dreams. Our foundation of this new house. Now, let's start where things began to go wrong. Your childhood.

When you were a kid, adults always asked, "What do you want to be when you grow up?" And wouldn't your answer always be something fun like a fireman, astronaut, policeman, or, in my case, Spiderman? The adult logic was, "You need to know where you're going before you can get there," and the kid logic was simply a feeling of, "I wanna do something fun. I just want to be." Both tracks of reasoning have a lot of merit. And your answers as a child probably pointed to your true self.

Somewhere along the way you actually do grow up and seem to forget your child logic. One day you're sitting at your desk or on a job site just counting down the minutes to the end of your day and thinking, "How did I get here?" The answer is simple. You forgot to ask and answer the age old question: "What do I want to be when I grow up?" Instead, you started asking and answering the question: "What's the best thing I can do to get a well-paying job?" or "What can I do to make me fit in?"

Living a dream life is not about fitting in or just getting a job. It's about having a passion, doing what you love and having fun. It's about making your own decisions about what is best for you, like you did when you were six years old. Except this time you don't need to listen to other people when they say, "You can't do that." It's about life with no limits. The urban dictionary definition of funemployment says, "The condition of a person who takes advantage of being out of a job to have the time of their life." I'd like to take it a step further and define it as, "The condition of a person who takes advantage of their strengths and passions to create a job where they have the time of their life."

The next step in creating your dream life plan entails taking action with the end in mind. You were given a body for a reason. And it wasn't so you could sit on your ass and watch TV all day. Or, for that matter, sit in front of a computer screen wishing you were somewhere else. Your brain and body were built to realize your dreams. For what is the point of a dream unless expressed and realized? You playing small and not listening to the voice of the universe will only lead to pain. When you truly decide to do something about a dream, all sorts of amazing things are presented to you that you would never have thought possible. Even at this very moment, as I write this, I'm in awe of this truth in my life every day. The majority of this book has been and will be written in Tulum, Mexico in house number seven. I wasn't sure why Ingrid and I had booked a ticket to come here until this book started expressing itself. An experience that would not have come to fruition without first accepting my assignment from the universe to write the book—an idea that came to me from a still place. This type of universal handout is something I have come to have faith in. "Jump and your life will appear" is only scary if you think about it too much.

Returning home from Calgary on a high from the Breakfast TV success I discussed previously, I was now faced with the prospect of "what next?" How was I going to take this burning desire and turn it into a life worth living? Having already started and sold a successful business helped me understand the people, product, and promotional processes needed to make this dream an ongoing reality. Manifesting your dream, wishes, and desires is a balancing act. The personality you have created to date has been molded primarily by an ego-focused society, whether you realize it or not. Now is the time when we begin to use our minds to implement our dreams. But it's all too easy to fall out of the zone.

My desire to help people overcome their pain by granting wishes imprinted the dream of a wish-granting road trip on my mind. When it came time to begin planning the action steps needed to make this a reality, I began with the end of the road trip in mind. I imagined how it would feel to be sitting in Miami after two months of wish granting, sipping a mojito with friends and talking about genie adventures. I imagined how it would feel to see the looks on the faces of the people I surprised along the way. I imagined looking at photos, newspaper stories, and videos of the wish granting. From this point of feeling, I worked backward, outlining the things that needed to happen now to reach this point of fulfillment.

One of the most important things I learned in business was to not go too far down a road without seeing something beautiful along the way. In other words, don't continue with a losing idea. A desire or dream you think is coming from God may in fact be coming from your ego. Or even more likely, you may be implementing this divine idea from an egotistical state. I know; I've been there. If this is the case, your dreams may never reach the manifestation stage. To help ensure the pain associated with this egotistical mistake isn't too severe, I recommend thirty-day (at most) tests for all your ideas. If you don't see progress in these thirty days, go back to your initial dream. Revisit the feelings associated with it. Are they presently being fulfilled? Why not?

I've had many ideas that never manifested because they couldn't pass the thirty-day test. But like Wayne Gretzky says, "You miss 100 percent of the shots you don't take." Get into the practice of taking shots from different angles until you find your groove. And don't be afraid to let go of a dream if it isn't serving you. You're evolving with each one. Remember, life's a journey, and it's only through experience you'll learn what matters most. Rule of thumb: if it doesn't matter, get rid of it.

Never forget that it's really right now that counts. Take a look at your thirty-day dream plan and list thing things you can do today. Procrastination in dream realization is a curse because the only reality is what is happening right now. The world is filled with talkers. Don't be one of those. Focus on action. Do yourself a favor—

put down this book right now, and list three things you can start and finish today that will be a stepping-stone to a fully realized dream idea.

Now that you have your thirty-day and daily action plan mapped, you'll need to look at these action items and find out how much they're going to cost you. This is the part of dream making where the majority of people fail—especially folks in the spiritual tribe. Bottom line, it's not something a lot of people feel comfortable with. And it is surely a whole lot more boring than dreaming. A lot of people enjoy thinking about their dreams so much that they forget action is needed. Let's face it, sitting on a couch daydreaming is a whole lot easier to accomplish in the moment. I've met many, many people in my travels who tell me they are going to be a New York Times best-selling author or change the world with a new big idea, only to see them the next year still in the dream phase.

Money or currency is simply a form of energy. Tapping into it will likely be crucial for your success. If your burning desire is strong enough and your dream fulfillment is at the top of your list of priorities, then ideas, people, and circumstances will come to you at the right time.

But before this can happen you need to price it out. You need to know what you need before you can ask the universe for it. How much will it cost to do the things you need to do to realize your dreams? Once you figure out the monthly cost, take it one step further and divide it by thirty to figure out the daily cash flow needed as well.

I want you to tattoo this on your mind. Say it over and over all day today and every day. "Money is great. Money is what I need to accomplish my dreams. It is OK to ask for money in exchange for service. I love what I do and deserve to get paid for it." Arguing with reality isn't something I find very beneficial, and while the universe is in control and cash may not be king, it's still important.

The next step involves becoming a perceived expert in your dream life. People believe in experts. They want to be close to them, learn from them. These experts' mastery and knowledge is always sought after. They are centers of influence and attract people to them. In the book Outliers, Malcolm Gladwell says it takes approximately ten thousand hours to become a master in a field. Lucky for you, I have a stepping-stone that significantly decreases this number. And while it may not make you an actual expert, it will begin to help with wish fulfillment.

There aren't many people dressed as genies roaming the world granting wishes for people in need. An expert, I reasoned, is essentially someone that people trust and who know a lot about a particular topic, with trust being the key word. So to become an expert, I would need to associate with people that other people trusted. Unfortunately, dressing up as an angry-looking blue genie isn't the easiest way to convince people to have trust in what you are offering. However, aligning with local news organizations across North America with a thirty-day dream day tour might just do the trick. Other options include reading best-selling books in the area you are interested in and aligning with experts via common goals.

The final step in transcending the illusion of limitations and creating your dream life entails believing in yourself and celebrating how far you have already come. Which may entail shifting the perspective on how you define success. Sitting on the edge of the bed, head in hands, weeping. That was the scene a few days after our first genie tour ended in Miami years ago. I was close to running out of my savings and couldn't see how it would be possible to continue granting wishes. With the thought of going back to a normal job after assuming I had found my calling being enough of a depressant to elicit the salty tears.

Fast forward seven years later, and while we've had our fair share of close calls when it comes to perceived failure, I've always made myself this one promise. If the genie is forced to stop doing what it does for lack of money or whatever, that's fine. What will be, will be. But it won't be a failure from my point to view.

Remember, our collective soul is infinite and cannot be quantified or qualified. Never let anyone define you, objectify you, or allow you to think that you are less than anyone else. We are exactly who we are meant to be in this moment. Moving forward, creating a path. There will be challenges, but they will pass. When these come up, take a deep breath and step into the metaphorical fire. Allow the flames to remove what is no longer needed, forging a stronger version. Realize that this moment, no matter what it is, is right on time. You've come a long way to get right here, right now. Respect your true identity, walking with grace no matter your life circumstance. Remember you are a spark in the vast story of the universe waiting to catch fire.

You are going to experience moments in the quest to realize your dreams that may feel like failure. But what looks like failure in one moment may become the best move you'll ever make.

Imagine going to the gym, coming home, sitting on the couch, and eating a beautiful salad filled with nutrients that will help your body grow. You're pretty pleased with yourself and your body in that moment, aren't you? There is a feeling of satisfaction at having pushed yourself to the limit and reaped the benefits of improved health, circulation, mood, and everything else associated with working out. Now change your perception. Imagine that you are a poor broken-down muscle in your body. That workout literally ripped it apart, and now it needs to repair itself. It mustn't be very much fun for that poor muscle. It has a lot of work to do. But that doesn't feel "bad" to you, does it? You know that it's leading to a bigger and better muscle. So, too, it is with your life. You are part of the whole universe. Part of the whole of God. When you are broken down, having just failed, remember: it's part of the plan. Everything that has ever happened is part of the plan. How could it not be? It happened.

Remember, most people don't even try. The fact that you have even reached the point where you are acting on your desire is huge! So give yourself a big pat on the back. But to really reach the stars you need to go that extra step, which includes a breakdown and breakthrough. You will need to accept failures as opportunities for growth, or guides on your path. You haven't come this far to only get this far. We all have our own path, and not everyone's looks like success from the outside world looking in. Pay no heed to that. Go with what feels best to you and let the critics have their say as you pass them. Everything you've ever wanted, everything you've ever needed is within, waiting for you.

When you give your gifts to the world, the world gives right back. Following your passions, you are energized by simply being who you are. Who you are destined to be. I haven't considered myself a writer since I was a boy. I'd always be writing stories then. Doing it just to do it. Never expecting anything in return, it was simply a way of expressing myself. I'd usually write, then draw some pictures to go with it. Looking back, I'm not quite sure when the stories stopped. Maybe they never really did. My imagination certainly didn't stop writing them. Over the past years I've been remembering the habit of doing what my dreams tell me to do. Following my passions. And writing has crept back into my life. It began with me wanting to write immediately after my morning meditations. At first I thought, "This is kind of weird." "I'm not a writer," I told myself. "Why am I doing this? What a waste of time." But a little voice kept whispering to do it. I began to listen. I began to write more and more, with the voice getting stronger and more confident each day. It told me to go to a writing conference in Florida with my friend Wayne Dyer. So I did. Then it told me to start posting on Facebook. Again, I listened.

Eventually, Wayne Dyer reposted one of my stories on his wall. It received over 5,000 likes and 1,500-plus shares. I spent the morning reading the comments of people who were touched by it. The voice said, "I told you so." And it brought tears to my eyes. I'm in awe of the power of listening to that little voice. Because when you listen, I mean really listen, it's the only thing you can hear.

Make today a blank slate. Forget about the things you've screwed up. They're already taking too much space in your head. Remember the dreams they've crowded out. You are infinitely awesome and pure. Remember that. We all screw up and always will. Accept it. Take your failures and learn from them. That's what they are for. Don't get too attached, because they aren't who you are. No one reaches the top of the mountain. We just go deeper into ourselves, remembering who we truly are. And there's one thing I can guarantee: thinking you're a "bad" person doesn't help.

Right now you might begin distancing yourself from the word failure. Instead, remember Thomas Edison's quote, "I have not failed. I've just found 10,000 ways that won't work." You are everything you are today because of the challenges you have overcome. Rise up and go find a few more.

What would you say are the chances of deciding to follow a dream and grant thirty wishes in three days for a Los Angeles-based family while filming for our pilot episode of The Genie, only to find out their number-one wish was to have their marriage vows renewed by Marianne Williamson—who just happened to have agreed, only days before, to work with us on a Canadian speaking tour? Add to this the fact that the very person that married them twenty years previously was—you guessed it—Marianne Williamson.

A month later would see us surprising them in Marianne Williamson's living room with their wish.

Such is the power of following your burning desires or dreams. Almost impossible synchronistic events appear to help guide you along your way. If you have the faith to jump with all your heart, listening to the altruistic voice of your soul, the universe conspires to take care of the details.

To see through the illusion of limitations, do the following:

1. Remember your passions by bringing back the kid in you. Life is meant to be fun, and putting yourself back in your child shoes will help you remember the "why" of your life.

2. Act with the end in mind. Imagining the feeling of having your dream realized today is a crucial aspect of wish manifestation. Get a dream book. Write down any inspirations as they happen. Don't just write down the idea. Write down every thought you have about it. Get it out on paper. It will help.

3. Bring everything into the now. List your top three wishes/dreams. List three things you can do today to help bring them to reality. List three things you can do tomorrow to bring them to reality. Do this every day and adjust accordingly. Read every night before you go to bed and every morning when you wake up, before your morning and evening meditations. Release your wishes into the silent space with the knowing they will bloom when the time is right.

4. Give any idea that has a burning desire a thirty-day test. You need to know when to hold them and when to fold them. Fail forward and begin to refine your dream-weaving craft.

5. Know how much it costs. Money is not a bad word, and you need it to realize most dreams. Accept the reality of this and begin to attract it to you.

6. Become an expert in your dream field. Associate with other experts, read inspirational expert advice daily, and remember that you are the average of the top five people you associate with

the most. List three people who can help you with your dream. Ask them to be a part of it.

7. Believe in yourself and celebrate successes. When you finish any project, specifically at the end of any thirty-day dream plan, go into creative incubation mode. Be still. Take some time off and do absolutely nothing. Give yourself time to listen to your heart. Review what's been done and ask yourself, "What could have been done better?" Now wait for your heroic spirit to tell you what to do next.

6

THE ILLUSION OF OWNERSHIP

The sixth of life's great illusions states that you can own things. Understanding that you can truly own nothing, not your body, house, car, land, this earth, its water, or the air you breath, will change everything. When Native American Chief Seattle was asked about property ownership his reply was, "We do not own the freshness of the air or the sparkle of the water. How can you buy them from us?" We've become spoiled, to the point that we think we own our ideas and dreams. We think we own the plan. And when things do not go as we visualized we become upset. Understanding that you truly own nothing will help you release your dreams into the world without any expectations, letting them grow and bloom in their own divine timing and unique way.

You can only lose what you cling to.

- Buddha

The irony of listening to a guided Deepak Chopra meditation so I didn't freak out leading up to I Am Genie's Deepak Chopra event on August 2nd wasn't lost on me. His calming voice was doing its intended job. Breathing slowed, thoughts drifted to whence they came, and eventually stress disappeared into being. With only a day left before the big day, I could feel the energy in the city changing.

Waiting in St. John's airport eight hours later, now without Deepak's soothing meditative voice, my thoughts wandered. What would the man Time magazine deemed one of the top one hundred heroes and icons of the twentieth century and "poet prophet of alternative medicine" really be like? What would I learn? Would he like me? Would we have anything in common? Would he be what I imagined? Were my guru-like expectations too high? Would I be disappointed? When Deepak finally appeared in comfortable clothes and signature red shoes, my first impression dashed expectations. Instead of seeing one of the most spiritually influential people on the planet, master of my guided meditations and a man who has written eighty-plus books, I locked eyes with a still, sweet, intelligent man. The type of man who embraced Jack Canfield's quote, "What others think about you is none of your business."

Getting to know each other while driving to the hotel, Deepak asked a few questions about the genie, nodding his head while keeping a very even keel as I spoke. Sometimes asking follow-up questions but mostly content to allow the conversation to merge into silence—instantly pointing out my egotistical habit of being uncomfortable in silence, especially with people I first meet or want to impress. Now, here with Deepak, this underlying nervousness came to the forefront. Second-guessing what I was saying, wondering if the right words were coming out, my speech began to ramble. Reminding me of a wish grant in Miami two years previously with CNN Hero Roy Foster. When I filled every silence with him, he very simply said, "You don't need to speak all the time, you know." These words rang in my ears, allowing the nervousness to subside. A little.

Carl Jung, one of the world's greatest teachers, eloquently states, "The pendulum of the mind alternates between sense and nonsense, not between right and wrong." Life is not a straight line with a beginning, middle, and end, as we sometimes like to think. It's more like the arc of a pendulum, as Jung noticed, full of moments leading to more moments. Each one dying before the next. In fact, you may have noticed that your stream of thought follows an arc, or, in other words, a storyline. Like that of a movie, with one thought feeding off the previous one, sometimes leading to the past, other times to the future. And your life, being a manifestation of this inner thought movie, is experiencing an ARC moment right now. At this very moment you have the amazing opportunity to either (A)ccept what these words are saying to you, (R)emove yourself from them and stop reading, or attempt to (C) hange them by altering the way you perceive what is being said. Understanding life from this positive ARC-focused perspective instantly puts you on the sense (rather than the nonsense) side of the pendulum and into the humble, gracious, powerfully fulfilling flow of life.

Nonsensical insanity ensues when we resist or reject the here and now, leading to unhappiness. Byron Katie encapsulates this with one sentence: "When you argue with reality, you lose, but only 100 percent of the time." In fact, most spiritual leaders throughout history repeat much the same thing. The father of Taoism, Lao Tzu, says, "Be content with what you have; rejoice in the way things are. When you realize there is nothing lacking, the whole world belongs to you." And Deepak's thought on the subject? "Nothing brings down walls as surely as acceptance."

After dropping Deepak off at his hotel, I felt a little disappointed in myself. I had allowed my expectations to bring me to the nonsense side of the pendulum, clearly taking me from the flow. For those fleeting moments driving from the airport I wasn't allowing Deepak to simply be. Instead of flowing with reality, my words attempted to force him into a preconceived role of who I thought he should be. Why didn't he talk more? Why did it seem like he didn't really care what I had to say?

My mind began to play tricks on me as I looked for him to fulfill an imaginary role I had created. I made conscious note to be more accepting of Deepak's unique, still being. The following morning I arrived at the Sheraton to escort him to an interview. From across the hotel lobby, I noticed him sitting at a long table, eyes closed, deep in meditation. How could he so effortlessly achieve this state in the midst of so many people walking about, frantically talking? Tapping him on the shoulder brought with it a big smile and hug. Today already felt different. I had changed my perception to one of sensible acceptance and began to notice that Deepak was teaching me without saying a word. The silence in the elevator on the way to the interview felt perfect. Consciousness was shining its light into the moment, establishing a quiet bond between me and this intensely interesting being.

The remainder of the day saw me at the venue ensuring everything was going according to plan. And with an event like this, nothing ever fully goes according to plan. The same would hold true for the evening. In the past, altered plans combined with my unwillingness to accept reality caused unhappiness. Such is the scorn you create with the unholy love of expectations. My hope in this experience was to stay conscious and watch myself. My desire to ensure everyone was happy with the show caused an ache when I saw various things not going as I would have liked. Throughout the night, whenever I began to let my thoughts and expectations control me, I'd just breathe. Take a step back from the drama and put things in perspective. Be still. Like Deepak.

The first way you can see through the illusion of ownership is to accept every moment you find yourself in. This includes accepting people, situations, and words you may not presently agree with. Expectations are a result of becoming attached to an outcome, which, more often than not, isn't going to manifest exactly the way you've visualized. My relationship with Deepak had gone from "expecting Deepak" to "accepting Deepak," effortlessly opening the path to evolved happiness, reminding me of the Hafiz quote: "Even after all this time the sun never says to the earth, 'You owe me.' Look what happens with a love like that; it lights the whole sky." Be sensible, and don't argue with reality. Forget the words reject and resist. Flow with life's natural ARC, and positively (A)ccept, (R)emove yourself, or (C)hange any situation that comes your way. And above all else, be the light.

This doesn't mean you can't intend for things to happen in your future. That's what dreams are for. The key to seeing through the illusion of ownership is to intend and detach, essentially casting your wishes and desires into the infinite space of existence to be fulfilled by the universe's infinite organizing power, of which you are a small and crucial part.

After reading the book The Power of Intention by Wayne Dyer, I felt as though it was only a matter of time before we met and became friends. It became an intention of mine to follow this desire through, and when I noticed he was going to be in Detroit at the same time we were scheduled to have a dream day there, we organized for the person we intended to surprise to go to his lecture. I was super excited to finally meet this amazing man. So you can imagine my surprise to wake up to an e-mail from our dream day sponsor saying, "Sorry, Josh, the dream day is cancelled," on the day I was scheduled to fly to Detroit.

When I received this e-mail I felt my spirit had let me down. Why would I get this knowing feeling only to be let down at the last moment? There was a time when I would have let this feeling overcome me, dwelling on the hardship and bad luck I had. Instead, after the initial shock, a deep calm came over me. I saw it as the universe guiding me to where I was meant to go. I went inside myself looking for the lesson in it. Almost immediately my spirit presented me with an idea. If you can't go to Wayne Dyer, why not have Wayne Dyer come to you? Instead of sulking, I continued to follow my heart and sent an e-mail to the head of public relations for Hay House who was helping organize the dream day, with my proposal to bring Wayne to Newfoundland.

After pressing send, I forgot about it, trusting that whatever happened would be best. But I sure did have a good feeling about it. We soon got a response to contact Wayne's assistant, Maya. I called right away. I remember hearing her voice for the first time and thinking, "I love this woman." We hit it off immediately, joking and having fun on the phone. She told me she would look into having Wayne come to Newfoundland but couldn't make any promises as he gets so many requests. I followed up with an e-mail request and went about my genie business, granting wishes and barely staying afloat for most of that year. But it didn't seem to be the same struggle as in the past. I was learning from it, looking for the lessons instead of being hurt by them.

Now I'm not saying it was easy, always wondering if the genie was going to survive. Life has a way of bringing you down when you need to pay the bills. The faith was there, but my conversations with God were becoming more animated the harder things got. By January 2013, I can remember being at my boys' house reading Conversations with God, by Neale Donald Walsh, again wondering where the money was going to come from to pay for all my responsibilities and mounting debt. I remember crying and screaming, "Help me, God damn it! Help me!" I broke down, silently weeping and wondering.

The next day, I received this e-mail from Wayne Dyer's assistant, Maya:

Hi Josh,

I think he will do this but I'm out of town till Feb 8th and wonder if I can confirm at that time? Hope all is well with you,

Maya

By April we had a deal. Dr. Wayne Dyer was coming to Newfoundland. My spirit rejoiced. Help was on its way. The rest of the year began to feel like a dream, with everything seemingly just fitting into place. A flower blossoms when God tells it, as does most plant life—a happy dance of balance between nature and nurture with no expectations. Nature doesn't expect. Humans do. Our ability to be conscious of our surroundings and the free will associated with this has put us in a class different from most of our earthly counterparts. It is an ability that has separated us from the rest, where we have seen ourselves as superior because of it. But it's disconnected our flow in many ways, not the least of which has been the expectations we place on our environment. We expect our children to develop certain skills and abilities in a certain time frame via school, and if they don't blossom the way we say and in the timing that suits us, we call them failures. If a child doesn't follow in his or her father's footsteps or according to our definition of success—again, failure. Or if your spouse doesn't show you affection in the way you like, you may reserve your love for a time when it suits these expectations. But imagine a world without expectations where, like the flower blooming on that perfect spring day, you were encouraged to do the same, listening to your inner guidance for the divine timing. No pressure, just perfectly being who you are in all your splendor.

The third way you can see through the illusion of ownership is ask yourself the following whenever the world seems to be going against you: "Is my thought on this topic true?" The truth is, whatever has happened to any of us was supposed to happen. You know how I know? Because it did. The story you make up to deal with it doesn't change that. I realize acceptance of your life situation isn't always easy, especially when you may have very real physical issues to deal with. But, know this: it is possible. When life gets you down and you don't see any way out, you may want to read this quote by Henry Ford that helped me recently: "When everything seems to be going against you, remember that the airplane takes off against the wind, not with it."

To see through the illusion of ownership, do the following:

- Intend and detach. Intending for your dreams to become a reality is the easy part. Most people get caught up so much in wanting their dreams to materialize that they continue wanting. Allowing your dreams to bloom when they are ready is often overlooked and crucial.

- Accept. Look for the lesson in every experience. Things that may look like failures today could become your biggest successes tomorrow.

- Ask yourself if your thoughts on a subject are absolutely true. Couldn't you potentially be wrong or only partially correct? Is there something you are doing that can be adjusted?

7

THE ILLUSION OF TIME

The seventh and final of life's great illusion states that time exists. Looking beyond the clock, we come to realize that time doesn't hold up to the light of our truest reality. Being able to see through this greatest of illusions will render all remaining hardship, struggle, and pain powerless.

Time isn't precious at all, because it is an illusion. What you perceive as precious is not time but the one point that is out of time: the Now. That is precious indeed. The more you are focused on time—past and future—the more you miss the Now, the most precious thing there is.

- Eckhart Tolle

People that are truly in the moment have an energy that draws you to them. Eckhart Tolle certainly had this. When I greeted him at his car as he arrived at Queen Elizabeth Theater, he asked me to join him after the sound check. As we sat in the green room, truly meeting each other for the first time, we discussed topics that ranged from the root of fear to the evening before us. And all the while I had the sensation that as he spoke he was also watching himself at the same time. His awareness giving him a larger than life presence. With only fifteen minutes before I was set to go on stage and introduce this beautiful man, I felt no fear or thoughts of my upcoming task in front of twenty-eight hundred people. Replaced, instead, by a wonderful conscious connection between us. The next two hours would see Eckhart speak about the power of now with as much humor and compassion as I've ever seen. The audience was in rapture and you could hear a pin drop. No coughing, no cell phones, just the silence of Eckhart's magnetizing and powerful words. I watched most of it from the side of the stage, time standing still.

We've come full circle on this topic of magic and have now reached the central and grand master of illusions: time. Luxuriously wandering to this part of the story, we are now ready to rise above it by gaining a clearer understanding of what your purpose in life is. Every aspect of this universe has a purpose. Much as an acorn's purpose is to grow into an oak and a caterpillar's is to become a butterfly, each person in this world has a purpose to fulfill. The sooner you realize what yours is, the happier and more fulfilled you will become. Some people naturally flow into their mission at a young age, gliding through life in bliss. For the majority of us, it's more of a slog, with two steps forward and one step backward.

The first way to transcend the illusion of time is to practice always having an awareness of your true nature while going about your everyday tasks. When you speak to Eckhart, his practice of this is palpable, creating a true space affecting anyone who has the pleasure of being in his presence. A practice that can be cultivated in you. Previously, we talked about the importance of realizing you are a spirit having a human existence during closed-eyed meditations. Here we take that realization a step further, and do so while being in the world. Some techniques to help you with this process include walking meditations and practicing changing your perspective from a tense-eye focus to one where you see the world from your heart center.

When looking out into the world, take your focus away from your eyes, allow your brow to relax, and shift the perspective to a space in the middle of your brain, or the hypothalamus gland. This will become your meditative anchor. Now attempt to view your surroundings from this perspective. Instead of straining your eyes to look out into the world, relax your brow and view the world from this space in the center of your head. Francesca McCartney calls this the meditative sanctuary, and the practice can be transformative in developing a connection with space while going about your daily tasks.

The iconic monk Thich Nhat Hanh has made walking meditation much more popular in the West recently, and it is one of the best ways to bring spirit into conscious doing. I first began practicing it during my morning meditations on Signal Hill in St. John's, Newfoundland overlooking the water as the sun rose. During my three- to four-minute walk to a meditation spot on the north side of the hill, I would become conscious of every step I took, made easier by the fact that early in the morning there would always be snails on the path. Conscious not to step on them, I imagined myself avoiding lotus flowers that I didn't want to hurt. Making each step a practice in mindful concentration, I'd feel the earth beneath me, as I accepted its energy into my body and merged with it. Steps would be slow and precise, with no thought of going or coming, all concentration reserved for each step. It's very important to practice this in a slow, methodical, mindful way. The goal is to release yourself from your thoughts and become one with the now.

Being in nature is one of the best ways to reconnect with spirit because the magnificent energy of the trees and water can overshadow your thoughts, helping you merge back into truth. This is why, whenever I can, I have walking meetings to discuss business. Ingrid and I also do this every morning, and it helps us stay connected while planning for the future.

Another practice to transcend the illusion of time is to begin to do more of what you love. Have you ever noticed that when you are doing what you love, you lose track of time? This isn't an accident. It's because time is only a concept directly linked to thought, and when you are doing what you love, you break these imaginary boundaries. The challenge is that when we grow up, most of us forget to do what we love. Working long hours to keep the bills paid has a way of messing things up. But you can change that by putting the focus back to where it counts. Make a list of the things you love to do, and begin carving out more time to do them in your everyday life. They may be as simple as playing a sport you love or as profound as switching careers entirely. Let spirit guide you.

Escaping the illusion of time entails choosing to love fear in as many moments as possible. Paulo Coelho points out in one of my favorite books, The Alchemist, "There is only one thing that makes a dream impossible to achieve: the fear of failure." Let's reset our fears, and bring the music back to our ears.

Saying things like, "I can't do that, I have too many responsibilities" is a cop-out. The fact of the matter is, you're happy in your bubble, even if it's slowly killing you. Fearful thoughts poison you, releasing cortisone into your body. When humans were running around as hunter-gatherers, fear served us well. Preparing us for fight or flight, eliciting an adrenaline rush which gave our bodies big shots or cortisone, tensing muscles, increasing our breathing, and intensifying our heart rates. This instinct was very helpful if a saber-toothed tiger was about to jump on you, but not so much these days. Today our fear is rarely used to avoid a potentially life-threatening situation. So when your mind tells your brain it should fear something, it can't tell the difference between the saber-toothed tiger and the fear of potentially failing an exam or not performing well at a sales presentation. The fearful thought triggers the cortisone, which is essentially poison to your body. It's not meant to be used regularly throughout the day. When it is, your body simply can't handle it, and it causes deterioration, leading to diseases, both physical and mental.

I'm assuming you don't want to live in fear

and would love to move away from its hold on you. The solution is deceptively simple. Change your reaction to your thoughts. Or as Wayne Dyer liked to say, "Change your thoughts, change your life." I'm a fairly shy and solitary person. The primary reason I put myself out there is to inspire others, which tends to bring me into the spotlight. There was a time when having to give speeches scared me to the point where I constantly avoided situations that might put me on a stage. When I was set to give a TEDx speech it was a different story. I had decided to face my fears, but they were still there. It entailed running out on stage as the genie, jumping on a big red X before quickly taking off my mask, and beginning the story of how my father passed. It was the first time since becoming the genie that I had to remove my mask and give a speech, and I found it daunting. Add to that, the subject matter was intensely personal, much like this book. I had been practicing the speech with the help of the TEDx organizers for weeks, and would always mess something up. I just wasn't feeling it, and with every screw-up, more fear set in. Until the night before the event.

I was blessed with the opportunity to sit with another of the speakers, a German Holocaust survivor from the Second World War. His story was horrifying. That night he gave me his book and I read it cover to cover before going to sleep. When I woke up the next day, I remember having a new thought about the presentation. "What's the worst that's going to happen?" I asked myself. People might come up to me and tell me I did a good job even if I didn't. Not exactly a wild animal chasing me.

The night of the presentation I felt a peace I hadn't felt before. After a quick meditation, I slid a photo of my dad in my pocket before hitting the stage. Ten minutes later, a standing ovation. I remember being surprised when everyone started clapping, because during the entire speech I felt Dad watching me. It was surreal. When everyone began to clap, I came back with a jolt of surprise, knowing I had solved a little piece of life's puzzle.

I realized then that in any given moment, you have the divine responsibility to love fear. I realized that while danger can be very real, fear is, without a doubt, a choice. And if fear is expressed in situations that aren't dangerous, then it doesn't serve anyone, least of all yourself. If you lived on the surface of the sun or in the midst of light, would you know anything of darkness? So it is with love and fear. Ask yourself which feels better. Now direct your attention to it. Like your ancestors, with fear, you can choose to fight or flee. But there is another way. Shine a light on the fear. Understand it. Question it. Love it. Use it to propel you to greater heights than you can imagine.

To see through the illusion of time, do the following:

- Do more of what you love. Get in the zone.

- Be while doing. Go to your meditation sanctuary.

- Choose to love fear. A loving embrace has the magical power to dissolve any challenge. Let it be your magic, now and forever.

TINY BOOK OF MAGIC REMINDERS

G o within and you won't go without. Have walking meetings. Work for ninety focused minutes, then take a break. Twenty-second hugs rock! Watch for synchronicities. The power of now attracts things and people to you. Ride the wave. Reconnect with your childlike self—no ego. Don't make decisions based on fear or greed. The mind is powerful enough to cause blisters—manage your mind. Value every encounter in your life, and treat all people as your teachers. Choose love over fear.

Never give up on your dreams, no matter how silly. Most dreams take five years. We are not alone. Out of pain come the greatest teachings and opportunities for growth. Realizing this allows you to transcend pain. Your spirit can heal anything. People are doing the best they can with what they have. Following the herd has caused some of greatest atrocities in the world and is one of the biggest causes of unhappiness in the world—we are all distinct lights and need to follow the voices in our hearts. Go with the flow. Detach from the outcome.

The greatest people in the world fail regularly. We are all one, and everything is connected. Never look a gift horse in the mouth. Giving and receiving should be balanced—to not accept gifts throws off this balance. Treat everyone as divine even if they don't deserve it. We are brainwashed into believing we are our identity, whether it be a jock, nerd, prep, beauty queen, or rocker. In reality, we are all divine extensions of one source. Don't die with your music still in you. The wake of a boat doesn't affect its future course. Angels are real and aliens exist.

Don't rely on your five senses; use your spider sense. When faced with a decision, ask, "Am I doing this from fear or love?" Don't look for approval. Fit together the pieces you are given. Find a special place to be alone for at least fifteen minutes each day. Watch animals and nature carefully; they'll teach you things. Every day is a little life—treat it like one. Forgiveness will change your life. Ask "How may I serve?" instead of "What's in it for me?" Change your perception if it's causing you pain. Baby steps lead to giant leaps.

Align yourself with a higher version of you by following your passions. Stop shit-talking. Create a bucket list and set intentions to complete the items on it by specific times. Do something you fear once per day. Everyone suffers; if you can find meaning in the experience it can become a triumph instead of a tragedy. Read something inspiring every day. You are part of a gigantic puzzle. Don't try to fit in by changing who you are because it won't work_you're already perfect. Remember that. Be wary of those who know better. Tell the truth, even if it's unpleasant.

You are a spirit unrestricted by time, space, or your physical condition. Don't argue with reality; create reality. Live as though your dreams are already a reality, and don't chase them; will them into being. We are all geniuses; society makes us less than our truest self. Actions, feelings, and love mean more than words. You'll see it when you are ready. Stop making excuses. Help people who feel they are alone realize that they are not. Consciousness is contagious and lifts the spirits of those around you. Banish doubt. Practice being the witness to your life. Shut down inner dialogue.

Be selfless. We were given a body for a reason—use it. Don't assume another's truth is yours. The shift: if 3.14 percent of the population champions a new practice, idea, or way of being (like consciousness), the rest of the population follows suit. The hundredth monkey. I am not my DNA. Be a fire-starter. Is the thought you are having absolutely true? How do you know for sure? What if it's not? Who would you be without it? Choose your words wisely—"I have an ankle injury" has a different energy than "my ankle is healing." Be careful what you say after the words "I am." It's not about what you want but what you are. We are all part of different tribes and cults; awareness of this helps us escape the dogma. I am Canadian—good or bad statement?

Reclaim your divinity. The ego relishes pain, and without it would cease to exist. The real magic of wish granting happens when you shift from wanting to be someone or have something to being who you are. Align with God-consciousness and all else follows. Love what you fear. From the moment we are born we are trying to get back to spirit—our original nature. Be the light. Let love be your magic. Let your fun out. I am that I am.

JOSHUA DAWSON

WISH GRANTER| AUTHOR | PRODUCER

Joshua born 1974 is an accomplished genie, entrepreneur and founder of I Am Genie, an inspirational wish granting movement.

 Lives on magical Galiano Island in British Columbia with his fiancé Ingrid.

 Granted hundreds of wishes in over 100 cities across North America. TEDx Presenter.

 Loving Dad of his beautiful Inspirations Jack and Hugo.

 Graduated with a Bachelor of Commerce from Memorial University.

 The Tiny Book of Magic: A Genie's Guide to a Wishes Fulfilled Life released in 2016.

 He believes that "The world is full of magic if you know where to look."

MAJOR MILESTONES

2010

A Genie is born. Beginning a 6 year journey on the road granting wishes to inspiring people in need.

Winner of "New Producer to Watch" at Cannes TV Festival MIPTV for Genie Reality Pilot.

2015

Inspirational events with spiritual leaders Eckhart Tolle, Wayne Dyer, Deepak Chopra and more.

Follow him day to day at

ABOUT THE AUTHOR

Joshua Dawson has been spreading magic across the world for over seven years. Inspired by the tragic and unexpected loss of his fifty-three-year-old father, Joshua initially felt that he had lost his anchor and longed to relive the days he and his father had spent loving life together. On a particularly dark day three and a half years later, a spark of magic touched Joshua's own life when he was inspired by an idea. While he might not be able to create more perfect days with his dad, he could bring them to others, thus igniting the release of a genie and a tidal wave of wish granting that continues today.

Having already inspired millions through over 250 media stories while granting hundreds of wishes, presented for TEDx on the power of love, filmed a pilot for a wish-granting TV series, and shared the stage with the world's greatest spiritual teachers, Joshua now sets his sights on releasing more magic into the world with the *Tiny Book of Magic: A Genie's Guide to a Wish-Fulfilled Life*.

CONTACT:

Joshua@iamgenie.org

www.iamgenie.org

facebook.com/experiencegenie

facebook.com/joshua.dawson

NOTES:

Made in the USA
Charleston, SC
06 December 2016